Growing Pains

poems by

Anastatia Caraballo

Finishing Line Press
Georgetown, Kentucky

Growing Pains

Copyright © 2024 by Anastatia Caraballo
ISBN 979-8-88838-459-6 First Edition
All rights reserved under International and Pan-American Copyright Conventions. No part of this book may be reproduced in any manner whatsoever without written permission from the publisher, except in the case of brief quotations embodied in critical articles and reviews.

ACKNOWLEDGMENTS

Dedicated to the memory of my abuela, Alexandra Caraballo, whose passing was the catalyst to birthing the majority of my work surrounding death and mourning. To her husband, my Grandpa Charlie, and to her son, my Uncle Jamie, both having passed during the pre-order period of this book. Reigniting the wound of loss. To my ancestors before me, to my friends and family who have passed too soon, to my wildly loving and inspiring children. Thank you to everybody who has emotionally held me during this time of grieving and simultaneously achieving this childhood dream of becoming a published author. And thank *you* for taking this leap of faith in picking up my book. My love and eternal gratitude goes out to everybody.

Publisher: Leah Huete de Maines
Editor: Christen Kincaid
Cover Art: Jennifer Reuter, Tanklady Creations. Instagram: @Tanklady11
Author Photo: Brittany Jean Stolp. Instagram: @bslovelypics
Cover Design: Elizabeth Maines McCleavy

Order online: www.finishinglinepress.com
              also available on amazon.com

Author inquiries and mail orders:
Finishing Line Press
PO Box 1626
Georgetown, Kentucky 40324
USA

Contents

Pobrecita 1

Inferno 5

Rolling Stone 6

Cancer Is 8

Wither 9

How to Build a Mother 11

Aries Sun, Capricorn Stellium 13

Conditions 15

Parallels 16

Inebriated 18

Three A.M. Liberation from Narcissistic Abuse 19

American Grand Opening 21

This is the Year I Turned 30 & Began Wearing Chokers &
    Crying to Baristas in the Starbucks Drive-Thru 22

Rise Above 24

Earth Wears a Veil of Mournful Lilies 26

Evergreen 28

Cursive Love 30

Dusk 31

Winter's Tendrils 32

Nirvana 34

Healing Bound 36

Pobrecita

CONTENT WARNING: SEXUAL ABUSE

"Pobrecita."

The only word mi abuelita is capable of uttering as three generations of her dis-eased family sit apprehensively in sterile hospital chairs.

My nervous forehead is gingerly stroked, timid yet loving, by Abuela's weary hand.

My mother sits on the other side of me, lacking the warmth my grandma exudes. Coolness pervades the space around her, making the ice pressed between my legs feel even more frigid.

Leaning into the security of abuelita's bosom, I attempt to ignore the loudness and chaos of the waiting room.

How can these other kids be laughing and so happy right now? It makes me so mad that I can't join them even if my center wasn't throbbing, blood trickling from too much movement.

My body was my last reminder of my age; everything else was already replaced by helping raise my siblings and taking care of all the chores and cooking with my Abuela.

Now I don't even feel like a kid anymore.

I try to find comfort within Grandma's face. She looks like a different person right now, maybe due to the harsh lighting, or maybe she's as scared as I am.

For the first time, her eyes don't convey monumental certainty and her short stature doesn't command respect.

Instead, on this day that surely must be a terrible dream, her dependable Downy clothes take on the stench of fear, worry, and most frightening of all: helplessness.

Guilt and responsibility weigh heavily on her defeated shoulders.

The abuse was supposed to stop with her.
Familial neglect, pain, thieving of innocence was supposed to end with her generation.

Instead, destruction, greed, and irresponsible lust have continued to permeate her gene pool.

This proud woman who can shut a man up with set lips and a raised brow now sits in her own bewildered silence.

This woman who one moment, can backhand so quickly at the utter of a curse word, and the next wrap those same disciplinary fingers around mine in silent apology, hums a familiar lullaby in promise to never lay hands on me again.

As my mother stands to ask a nurse for another ice pack, I sit cradled so tightly in Abuela's arm, as if I am her favorite stuffed animal.

Maybe she feels if I never leave her sight again, the world can no longer sink its wicked, gnarled teeth into me, rending flesh and childhood dreams.

A doctor calls me into the room to look me over. She is very kind and gentle, but she asks so many questions I start to feel like I'm the one in trouble…

Am I in trouble?

How much should I say?

He said if I told, they'd never
believe me and I'd be taken away.

"I don't remember," seems the safest response.
I know she doesn't believe me, but she removes the pressure from her questions and adds it inside me, instead.

Telling me to breathe, relax, trying to check my injuries.
"Focus on the Viewmaster. What's on the reel?"

I don't want to think about Goofy and Pluto playing and being happy.
I don't want to think about her poking and prodding, stretching me to stitch my wounds.

I don't want to think.

I wish Abuela could be in here, but the doctor says for my safety it has to just be me.

I am so embarrassed. My flower is supposed to just be for me, not for strangers to see.

After an eternity of having the most intimate parts of myself examined, I am ready to find refuge in Abuelita's arms. But her and mother are fighting again, this time in front of a police officer.

Everyone's attention is directed to the arguing Boricuan women causing a scene as I stand frozen, hoping for comfort.

This time I cry because there is no calm place to turn to. My nose runs since my feet can't.

My insides throb and I use all of the pain, confusion, and anger building up inside as a blanket. A shield, the only thing that seems to care about me.

Their backs turned, tempers flared,
this is not what I need right now.
I need togetherness,
I need stability,

I need safety.

I've never felt so exposed and so invisible at the same time.

Pobrecita.

Inferno

There was something unmistakable in mother's eyes.

On good days, two calm, cordial pools of amber gazed back at me.
But whenever I upset her, I could expect their rapid shift into violent infernos.

Dangerous flames reaching their fingers out to grasp my face.

Demanding, COMMANDING that I shut up and listen.
If I obey, the blaze retreats, leaving second-degree burns in their place.

But on the days where my anger and defiance combust into their own scorching rage,
her ancient, proficient fury digs its fingers into my deepest layers of skin, muscle, bone.

Leaving me charred.

Smothered.

Extinguished.

This is when her motherly instincts kick in. She tends to what's left of my blistered skin.

Does she understand that we can share the same fire?

Does she understand she's the one who reduces me to a pile of ashes?

Rolling Stone

Back in the elementary days, I used to dread Family Day.
Teachers asked, "Tell us about your sister, brother, mom, pets…"
They looked at me sympathetically, cautiously leaving out the space
for "father".

I don't even know enough about you to be called your daughter.
I don't know enough about you to responsibly love you or admire the
space you were supposed to hold onto.
Somehow, my grandparents had to replace you; instead of you
stepping up, it took two to recreate you.

And yes Daddy, it's because of you I've got those infamous issues,
drawn to dating older men, hoping to recreate what you were
supposed to do:
provide routine, stability, dependability, trust.
But in leaving, all you taught me how to do was chase passion and
lust.

I used to be filled to the brim with disgust. The moment anything
went wrong in a relationship, I'd be filled with mistrust.
Sure to the fact that my family history was repeating.
But see, in reality it was my trauma that kept me from succeeding.

Oh I *wish* I could be seven again.
When I thought your name was Merlin and it was fun to pretend
you were an famous wizard, in such high demand
that you were needed all over these Hollywood lands.

But now I'm 29, and I am way past the days of make-believe.
No more tricks up your sleeves; I know your name is marlin.
And I don't even have the emotional "in case of emergency" space left
to capitalize your name.

Childhood daydreams aside, I finally understand you're human.
You weren't off spreading magic, making dreams come true.
No, you had other families, giving me a dozen half-siblings,

half-relationships,
half-commitments,
half-way, bullshit apologies that aren't really apologies.

These are the memories you've left me with.
I can't even remember what you look like.
Is my hair kinky-curly like yours?
Does my kinky-promiscuity resemble yours?

And now, the first of all my siblings tells me you're dying.
Stage four kidney cancer, begin making amends since you're on your deathbed.
I can't be mad at her, she's got memories since she was your first family.
She doesn't understand that you've always been dead to me.

What the fuck am I supposed to do with that?
How the fuck am I supposed to feel?
I can't even deal.

I'm torn between losing the seed of my life and someone who was never real.

Cancer Is

the spider creeping along your veins, one stalking leg at a time
the precarious balance between not fully dead but not entirely alive

the un-saids taking space between your teeth
the chemical nightmare plaguing your daily routine

the regrets casting chilled shadows on weary heart

the hazy-fog dialogue you find yourself constantly speaking

the radiating aches that make your bones quake
minerals and nutrients evaporating with every sunset

the bucket list that sits unfinished
the anger at having made such a seemingly naive list to begin with

the famished vulture digging filthy claws into your shoulder—
each rivulet of blood a constant reminder that *any day can be your last*

the prescription cocktail that leaves you frail, a skeletal reminder of your healthier days

knowing the unknowns now dethrone the facade of everything you've ever known

the merciful days of sunshine rays when you can finally mean when you say you feel, *"okay"*

the what-if's you reminisce
the why-not's that replace them

the relentless acceptance of all that lies
underneath affectation's veneer.

> while there are many avenues to leave this soul path,
> cancer is the cul-de-sac where galaxies collapse.

Wither

Last night, I had a dream—
Well, it couldn't be a dream.
It was closer to a nightmare
where nothing was as it seemed.

I found myself inside a dilapidated hospital,
walls smudged with age and neglect.
The hallways had long been emptied;
I felt fear palpate my demolished chest.

I watched myself tip and toe and tremble
my way past rooms long abandoned by time.
Trapped essence of those who were birthed
and those who'd met their demise.

Unbeknownst to me, the dreamer,
I couldn't tell why I was here.
But my phantom doppelganger
was equipped with proper gear.

Propelled by predetermined mission,
she marched purposefully forward
while I watched, restrained somehow,
from above, mouth agape in horror.

At the end of this long corridor,
my feet found their way outside *his* door.
No who's or what's nor when's just, "*WHY?*";
brain chastised me down to my core.

My dad, her dad, our dad,
Lay broken beyond belief.
He was a vastly different version
than my childhood's memory.

Indecision, pain, and illness
permeated infected air.

I wished I'd had a mask on
for I feared my face would bare

the brutal honesty of my disdain.
How I wish I could remove his DNA-
from every atom, organ, artery,
and pretend I inherited another's veins.

The truth of this sordid matter:
Dad- I will never know you, but I love you.
Though forgetting is what I'd much rather,
I am only created in part to you.

These were the words that echoed in my broken head,
as astral me hovered near your broken death bed.

How To Build a Mother

Tell me, Mama,

when did it stop?
The candid photos without any plots
of random smiles, that tree in your favorite lot.
When did you turn from love to autopilot?

Tell me, Mama,

when did you waver?
That unshakeable joy we all loved to savor,
the way your laughter was the greatest flavor,
punctuating your sentences with effortless labor.

When did the stress of your life
begin to outweigh your heart?

When did the mission of finding a
husband become your priority?

I now understand you felt landing a man
was the best way to be loved and keep your
home in command.

But we didn't need a new replacement dad,

we just needed you.

Mama, why weren't we enough for you?

Mama…
Mama…

Mama, please remember that you once looked at me like I was a
blessing.
Please put the adoration back in your eyes despite your incessant
stressing.

I wish I could go back to that amniotic state of being,
when you felt pure excitement to meet your little jelly bean.

I need to feel like I am not your burden.

Can't you hear it in the faint stutters of my heartbeat?
Can't you see it when my eyes dim to a muddy brown?
Didn't you share this same fury about life not being fair?
Don't you remember when you shared this same defeated frown?

I want to forgive you, Mama.

Forgive you for learning as I learned,
as your firstborn, everything was brand new.
Forgive you for repeating as you were shown.
Forgive you for growing as I grew.

Because to be a mother is to embody forgiveness,
model unconditional love for her own children to see.

We all come from mothers.

I now know you, because I am you.

Aries Sun, Capricorn Stellium

You see my light, but my warmth is
so far away. Hidden away.
Glimpses escape. Beneath, buried
but not destroyed. I protect it.

I cherish it, mindful of whom
I let inside. For my fire, warmth
is not meant for all who seek it.
Not all deserve what I offer.

Warmth heals, fuels, lights throes of passion.
Gives sustenance, breeds creation,
sustains a life. But can destroy.
Sparks, inspires. But can spit fire,

venom bullets. Menacing curse?
Or honeyed words meant to nourish.
Choose wisely, for the depths of me
are not for all. My heart matters.

It opens wide—cozy, cordial.
Internal smile. When needed, heart
untethers swiftly, disconnects.
Cuts cords, stonewalls. Not to deny

entrance, light. Not to disengage,
hurt, dismiss you. Pretend you, we,
never existed. Not to make
you disappear, wane away, sad.

My only aim is to protect
my spirit, soul, energy, heart.
For now at last, I know my worth.
What I deserve, my value. Time

no longer tied, consumed with each
prospect, glimmer, each connection.
My energy is sacred. Pure.
I share that which I want. For my

needs, they matter. My heart matters.
I matter. Now I understand.
I open up when I'm ready.
I choose who I give my love to.

It has nothing to do with you.
You see my light, but my warmth is

so far away, tucked away, safe.

Conditions

> *Say you'll wait for me.*

Crooked toes dug into pin-needle sand,
beckoning me nearer with outreached hand.

> *Say you'll cradle me.*

Tucked neatly into the crook of your arm,
promise me refuge, ataraxis, warmth.

> *Say you'll lie to me.*

I'll wade closer to your desolate shores,
will my ears deaf to your mendacious roars

and to your obdurate ascertainment.
Just as you're blind to my tribulations;

comfortably numb to my trepidations.
Though I must ignore my indignations.

While trudging through your tepid ocean, it's
far too late when I remember that I

> *don't know how to swim.*

Parallels

I thought I saw you driving around town.

Precious oxygen was stripped from my lungs.
Ribcage seized, beyond intimidated.
Flight clearly outran any hopes of fight.

Unnerved down to my very synapses.
The way crude fear slithered around my heart,
on the cusp of strangling me into death.
He had always loved me so hard, it hurt.

But he never knew what love's essence meant.

Unrestricted love is not possession.
Unquestioning love is not obsession.
Divine love could never be repression.

Love should not feel like an anchor, dredging
your ship down regardless of your consent.

Dragging down to depths of uncertainty.
Tied to his current shipwreck destination he tries
talking up, begging you to ignore your instincts.

Release yourself from these unhealthy binds,
believe your sageness, don't question your mind.
Vigor, divine feminine dwells within.
You are not responsible for his sins.

I chant and repeat these affirmations.
Inhale deeply, self-convinced that could
not have been you. I exhale old pain.

I was berated, harassed, frightened, and
haunted in dreams and waking life. I left.

There's no possible way that was him, right?
I take a few right turns beyond the lights.
Old habits die hard when running from plights.

Inebriated

You are dark, melancholy whiskey. Robust barrel fire that
singes, roars, and scorches your way down my oblivious throat.
Unapologetic in every manner, from watering
my ignorant eyes to the way you make my tongue swell and choke.

Whether reeling me in with promises of mysterious
adventure, or the way you leave me emotionally broke,
I keep coming back to consume more of you. *Just one more drink.*
Energetically spent, chopped into logs of once-sturdy oak.

You embody the smoke that comes with a whiskey barrel's age.
You slosh over the crooked edge of my glass, leaving me soaked.
Seeing me in denial, my trust and tolerance building,
you light a blunt; making my flammability a grim joke.

Rapid pain sparks from an excruciating realization:
You never loved me. You just did not want to die lost, revoked.
Depression mixes with your whiskey and seeps through to my bones.
My grief is the foul scent of stale smoke that lingers unprovoked.

My heart beats past taxed anger, goes directly to bargaining.
You say you cannot be with me, for you are far too broken.
Maybe I can save you, so you might reconsider an "us."
Distraught, I know this can't be said, before I've even spoken.

I've absorbed numerous life lessons to keep you afloat, but
your uncertainty, fickleness, is not worth the hangover.
Though I initially chose to walk your downcast path with you,
your smoke is too smooth. *Now I remember why I stay sober.*

Three A.M. Liberation from Narcissistic Abuse

CONTENT WARNING: DOMESTIC ABUSE

And what am I if not thorough?

Severing this final cord down to bone,
gnawing through ragged, petrified marrow.

Sawing past the last layers of falsified cast stones:

Every derogatory name, insult you had attached to the guise of a sweet, toothache treat.

Every threatening message each time I tried to leave.

Every forceful act performed to satiate you and get me through another day lays here:

seared into my broken, brittle boneyard.

I am a mouse that got it's leg caught in your sticky glue trap,
lured into complacency by running my usual hidden escape routes.

Trusting my muscle memory to get me to safety,
but getting perilously stuck as I round the last corner to home free.

How did I make such terrible choices to end up here?

I chose to ignore intuition's "baseless" fears.

Now my body is immobilized but mind ferociously scrambles to find a way to save myself.

Unable to move yet acutely aware of your putrid presence,
refusing to reveal yourself but gleefully watching me fight for my life.

Fight or flight instincts on dire, daunting alert—
I did not think I could survive.

I thought for certain I would die at the hands of your morbid, masochistic manipulation.

You had aimed to make me weak, subservient, forcefully dependent on you

tried to break me of my stubborn Boricua willpower, grind my self-esteem and worth into withered flour.

Molding me into your sacrificial bread baked to bated outward perfection.

Somehow, inside is still completely raw. Carnivorous organs still beat, pulse, just beneath golden, obedient-facade surface.

You must be so fucking pissed.

Watching me escape from your surefire trap,
finally finding freedom from your poison grasp.

And though, for now, I am grievously injured,
I have broken free.

Rewarded with another chance to nurse my willing amputations, another chance to breathe new life tomorrow.

To learn from this relationship that would have ended me if I couldn't leave, leaving my children in eternal sorrow.

I have survived enough to escape with my life,

parts of myself missing, yet I am still alive.

American Grand Opening

Our bodies open.

Yawns escape slumbering joints
& muscles as we stretch side to side.

Another unspoken answered prayer:
we've awakened for another day.

For some reason, maybe blindly following the unbridled
laws of chaos, our hearts still beat uncertain palpitations.

Lungs still contract & expand against our will.
Against all understanding, neurons still fire away,
pinballing commands to the rest of our obedient bodies.

Fatigued limbs posing as arms raise above migrained heads.
Neck laterally snaps, crackles, & pops it's way to consciousness-

But now what?

Lead legs dangle off passionless beds.
Toes curl within too-warm socks, trying to lead
the charge into another square of our calendars.

Into perpetual busyness.

Minds falter, unwilling to continue blooming for menial work.

Stomachs churn, last nights uncomfortable &
necessary conversations sitting undigested.

Psyches shutters, decides to call in sick for a mental health day as our
bodies turn to autopilot,

open for business.

This Is the Year I Turned 30 & Began Wearing Chokers & Crying to Baristas in the Starbucks Drive-Thru

This is the year I stopped over-correcting my parking—
Rushing in, slowly pulling out, trying to find that sweet middle spot in the most unsatisfactory missionary fuck possible.

This is the year I stopped carefully practicing what I say beforehand. Let my sentences reflect the steaming plate of overflowing, undercooked scrambled eggs that is my brain.

This is the year therapy finally helps me become hyper-aware of all my traumas—yet I still actively decide to accidentally self-sabotage my relationships.
This time around, I have a clinical definition for it. *Same same, but different.*

This is the year I added a twist to my favorite old adage: if you don't have anything nice to say, don't say anything at all... & you don't have to go on an archeological dig to find something that may genuinely not be there.

This is the year Saturn, ruler of my natal chart, pats me awkwardly on the head & bestows upon me stereotypically unhelpful fatherly advice: "*You thought the first 29 years were rough? Keep your chin up. You ain't seen nothing yet.*" Guess all dads really must be the same.

This is the year I finally began learning how to take care of all of me & began unconditionally loving myself & remembering to practice what I preach: Love is not enough.

This is the year my therapist told me that humans are essentially walking conundrums & my ego put on a grand show performing another stage of death.

This is the year insignificance gracefully fell with blazoned autumn leaves but detriment held its unstable ground with ancient, stubborn roots.

Awareness doesn't make healing easier.

This is the year I turned 30 & began wearing chokers & crying to baristas in the Starbucks drive-thru & I'm still as lost as ever.

Rise Above

Why won't you try on these weary shoes?
I know they are defeated, barren, and destitute.
But these worn-down, earth-shattering blues
have sweat woven, determined miles by ancestors, resolute.

Won't you try on my tired spectacles?
I know they're crooked, smudged by migraine auras and ignorant skepticals.
They are bent, gnarled from incendiary anticipation
of another picnic lynching or public spectacle.

They no longer want to see, but we must bear witness to protect the truth.

What does all this mean to you?

If you're incapable, unwilling to walk in an oppressed's shoes—

then know there's an indiscernible line between you
and those who gleefully tie up murderous nooses.

What empathy must be lacked to turn an indifferent eye
to your fellow humans suffering—
souls shattered, famished, bruised from centuries of abuse?

What good is your voice if you don't speak for the unspoken?
What good are your hands if you don't use them
to help raise the fallen, the beaten down, the broken?

What good are your social media posts, "1 like = 1 prayer", "sending good vibes",
if you won't risk the comfort and security of your skin tones obscurity
to take up your oppressed humans' battle cries?!

These are people who daily must fight for their lives!
Each breath is a gift when everyday is filled with strife!

Be the change you proclaim to strive for in vain!
Strike down the indifference; fuck your niceties, get profane!
We all have the same bones and life force in our veins!
Walk a million miles with those in eternal cages and chains.

Earth Wears a Veil of Mournful Lilies

Mother weeps evaporated tears into surrounding constellations.
Fervor fever continues rising, atmosphere and stratosphere burning.

Rock mountain elders pose, groups of sacred threes
gazing out into the same coveted galaxies.

They wish to reunite and leave this squandered world behind.

Polluted sun rises to shed light on another massacre day—
Which country, which leaders, which volcanoes will explode today?

Canyons moan and groan at the sounds of war drones,
agonizingly weary of the fighting, the murders, the suffering.

Barren cacti spike and bleed rusted hopes.
Their subluxated spines break to greet the sun's rays.

Trying to uplift their humans to survive another day.

Trees cough, sputter sap, giving birth to sick saplings.
Saddened to provide their oxygen to a dying planet.

Upset that their unrequited sacrifice is in vain:

The foam-vein waves of hallowed seas,
those mesmerizing storms, gestating over dustbowl breezes.
Wonderstruck waves of electricity grazing skeletal trees.

Their humans in perpetually dire strife, ending others or their own lives—

None of it matters.

Glitter blankets glazing aquamarine, cloud peaks vocalizing,
gifting breath and shore-struck knees.

Waterfalls can only transform so much stagnancy,
turning churning volatile storms into deep-sleep yearning reprieves.

Evergreen

Storms like today remind me of Washington evergreens.

A steady rainfall,
peaceful background of treetops
dusted with eyelash dewdrops.

I allow my eyes to unyieldingly rest,
breathing in the perpetual mist, &
will my ears to mute all the chaos.

The steady beat of my heart travels back to eight years old,
my first memories of a peaceful childhood.

Of stable, consistent love.
Of reliable adults,
of dependable authority.

I am transported in the sighs, in the breeze of how a tree breathes.

I am reminded that security is a possibility.
I am reminded of a stable lifestyle,
all while developing my dreams.

All while unearthing my needs &
discovering my boundaries.
All while relearning how my soul needs reprieve-

Room to sprout from a seed to a sapling.

These are the muscle-memories that embrace me,
letting me know I need to have space to just be.

I feel it in each droplet that rolls from
blissful Ajna to smiling cheeks.

I'm reminded in watching rivulets of streams
traversing down to windowsills.

The way the dirt & pavement smells before a storm.
The way arm hairs raise to greet electrical undercurrent
permeating summer air.

I was born to commune with forests.
I was crafted to soak up Earth's feelings & memories
through open soul & soles of my journeyed feet.

I am meant to converse with the leaves,
to release the unserving unto the breeze.

Cursive Love

We were making more than love with our bodies, we were making promises.

Promises that seemed mere shallow words compared to the magnitude of beautiful sincerity pressed between us.

New stories etched their ways into fresh wrinkles created by our union. Tender kisses planted themselves on my pulsing neck, my blushing face, my smiling mouth.

My heart raced in anticipation as you hovered over me, one last tentative kiss before plummeting into pillow soft.

Our sweat-glistened bodies rocked in perfect rhythm. A symphony only we could fully appreciate.

Slow and patient. No demands, only innocent questions. Our eyes spoke truth over hushed words, mostly silent. Small moans escaped us as we continued the dance.

Pulling me on top offered new angles, a new ballad. We continued the rhythm all too perfect for us as the passion that began in the pit of my stomach overcame my entire being.

Moans and a rigid body let me know you're singing too. As we reached the crescendo, my heart stopped momentarily and my vision blurred.

Am I crying? I am not saddened, for we had just experienced something beautifully universal. We created that love together.

I lay my head on your chest, our heartbeats drummed a chant we weren't ready to verbalize yet:
> *Iloveyou, Iloveyou, I love you.*

Dusk

Dusk

Lies with familiarity
In between endless comfort, warmth
Between fields of distant echoes
Embedded compass points due North
Consciousness in muddled colors
And bleeding into hollowed trees
Higher you go, sun swallowed whole
Self-conscious blemishes of earth

Dusk

Blurred treelines, murky rivers find
The sanctuary of dimmed sight
Thin rays of sun, mini fireballs
Line with horizon's shapeless shades
Of purple, baby's-breath blue, blush,
Light clouds stretch like cottonwood trees
And mingle with birds, animals
Dark, protected from unsought eyes

Dusk

Shows of lightning bugs captivate
Us, who often take for granted
The grandeur of simplicity
Veil lifted, magickal stage
Between vivacious, timeless youth
Life flows fluidly, emphatic
And each passing shift brings about
Death of old patterns. Start anew.

Winter's Tendrils

in the unknown darkness

our irrepressible fears and traumas
have coercive power to manifest
from dense stones of worry in our stomachs
to violent palpitations in our chests.
dire fight or flight pumping, stuttering,
foreshadowing near cardiac arrest.

in the unknown darkness

anxiety gnaws our nails for us,
rushed panic commandeers the megaphone.
inadequacy quivers 'neath worn quilts,
reason hitchhikes on the side of the road.
unwarranted guilt turns to righteous rage
quiets down to indiscernible woes.

in the unknown darkness

its difficult to find our lost footing:
we curse, stumble, and are jostled about.
depression twines its tense roots around us,
we are scratched by broken branches of doubt.
worn down by ostensibly futile wars
within us, our tired fires fizzle out.

>>inhale<<

the sun slumbers often during winter,
vitamin D kisses a distant thought.
but if we create our own bright sunlight
we may be the spark in another's plot.

this is not meant to be our terminal ending,
we are not hopeless, desolate burdens.
morning will rise and embrace us once more,

bitter chilled days will fall off calendars
and very soon, we will be warm again.

< < e x h a l e > >

Nirvana

      They say Death has the most beautiful fields.
  He tends to them patiently, lovingly, producing the purest yields.

       Death's fertile soils owes its vast nourishment
    to every recycled body's inevitable refurbishment.

      Death is hospitable, appreciative of all who arrive,
  he wastes nary a mineral nor organ so his fields may thrive.

       He is a sentry, a safeguard between realms,
    as dependable and cyclical as his sacred Elms.

      But he cannot speak. To express his gratitude,
  Death gifts forget-me-nots in a welcoming platitude.

His milky lilies dance on embracing breeze.
Hush and you'll hear, "*I will always love you,*"
from blushing orchids and bees.

Aloe is sewn by affection and born of grief.
Pink carnations promise, "*I'll never forget you,*" such cherished relief.

Lotus flowers bloom in hopes of rebirth and self-regeneration,
alabaster hyacinths offer prayers and undying dedication.

Willows weep with you, as you adjust to life hereafter,
marigolds find despair in their mirthless laughter.

Bedded sanguine poppies tremble in excitement, waiting to greet
your soul.
Ivory roses recognize renewed innocence, ready to console.

These acres of floral fields are ample substantiation,
that our flesh is temporary but our immortal souls are for the ages.

What is our fate, if not being born to die?
To courageously and vivaciously
cherish every moment you breathe life?

To perish on some predetermined day,
to nourish Death's backyard,

To find solace in knowing your beloved
ones are forever tethered to your heart.

Death culminates eternal patience, ever
ready to welcome your divine essence,

Your life has always been an everlasting gift;
these fields realize your empathic omnipresence.

Death frees you of a recycled body
so you can bloom

anew.

Healing Bound

weeping willows lend their leaves to me,
leaving me in pause and clarity.

Luna's illusions are not lost on me
for lost things are rarely as they seem.
dreams are rarely trapped in root-bound seams,
spilling into wake as brief reprieves.

weeping willows lend their leaves to me,
leaving me in grief and clarity.

such wicked things from my shadows creep,
pleading release from within my deep.
relentless nightmares are bound to be
the very reason which willows weep.

begging clemency from root-bound sleep;
if our traumas are freed, they can breathe
so sunlight and growth may be retrieved.
we heal in rich soil—old pain is cheap.

weeping willows lend their leaves to me,
leaving me in peace and clarity.

Anastatia Caraballo is a poet, licensed massage therapist, and a mamabear of two curly-haired wildflower children and two furbabies. Born in Burbank, California, life has taken her all over the West Coast and Midwest. She has been writing poetry and short stories since age 8 and loves to learn and experience all that life has to offer, including studying abroad, reading Tarot, making herbal compresses, and being a self-taught bass guitar noob. Through all of life's adventures, she has digested a plethora of lessons, blessings, and experiences, word vomiting and processing them through the catharsis of writing and therapy. Her work delves into the abyss of mental health, including eating disorders, self-harm, familial strife, grief, purpose, and what it means to be a human.

www.ingramcontent.com/pod-product-compliance
Lightning Source LLC
Chambersburg PA
CBHW020220090426
42734CB00008B/1149